Schriften des Münchner Centrums
für Governance-Forschung

herausgegeben von:

Prof. Dr. Hans-Bernd Brosius
Prof. Dr. Karsten Fischer
Prof. Dr. Edgar Grande
Prof. Dr. Carsten Reinemann
Prof. Dr. Bernhard Zangl

Band 5

Stephen M. Maurer

Regulation Without Government

European Biotech, Private Anti-Terrorism Standards, and the Idea of Strong Self-Governance

Nomos

Die Deutsche Nationalbibliothek verzeichnet diese Publikation in der Deutschen Nationalbibliografie; detaillierte bibliografische Daten sind im Internet über http://dnb.d-nb.de abrufbar.

Die Deutsche Nationalbibliothek lists this publication in the Deutsche Nationalbibliografie; detailed bibliographic data is available in the Internet at http://dnb.d-nb.de.

ISBN 978-3-8329-7093-2

1. Auflage 2012

Foreword

Regulation Without Government is an important albeit provocative contribution to the current governance debate. Scholars have traditionally assumed that regulation requires a strong and powerful government. Public regulators, the argument runs, must be able to force market participants to pursue regulatory goals. If they do not, business will resist. Stephen Maurer paints an entirely different picture: He convincingly shows that voluntary standards set by the market participants themselves can sometimes be remarkably mandatory. Under certain circumstances, at least, self-governance can be much stronger than we normally assume.

Maurer speaks from personal experience. In 2009, he helped companies that manufacture artificial DNA to draft and adopt a groundbreaking new Code of Conduct. This Code has been widely praised for its comprehensive list of actions that companies must take to examine customer orders – and the customers themselves – before selling DNA that could potentially be used to make biological weapons. The story is even more remarkable because the industry is diverse. Indeed, two large companies initially opposed the Code and tried to replace it with a much weaker and less expensive alternative. Despite this, more than eighty percent of the industry had endorsed the Code or a substantially similar document within three weeks. This figure even includes the same companies that originally tried to derail the initiative. Even more surprisingly, the Code turns out to be significantly more ambitious than the US government's official guidelines.

The idea that private standards can be more demanding than government ones challenges our most basic assumptions about regulation. This makes it fitting that Maurer should have presented this work as the first installment in a new "Contract Governance " lecture series here at the Munich Center on Governance, Communication, Public Policy and Law. Contract governance scholars use insights from governance theory and contract law to explore, for instance, the impact of contractual arrangements on government. Maurer's work shows that contract governance can yield impressive results and that private self-commitment can be a very effective tool of regulation. As such, it could lead to new approaches in our perennial search for regulations that avoid unnecessarily intrusive burdens and unintended consequences. For this reason, the present publication – and Contract Governance research in general – may also help to preserve individual freedom.

This contribution and the "Contract Governance" lecture series in general have been made possible by generous funding of the VolkswagenFoundation. They form part of the academic activities of the respective Schumpeter research group, based at the Munich Center on Governance and at the Humboldt-University of Berlin.

We are grateful to Stephen Maurer for coming to Munich and contributing this lecture. We also wish to acknowledge Karl Riesenhuber, who not only helped to arrange the talk but served as a dedicated discussant and contributed many invaluable comments. Finally, we wish to thank Markus Fischer (Entelechon GmbH) for providing his first-hand insights into how the Code was organized.

Munich, August 2011

Florian Möslein
Schumpeter-Fellow

Contents

Regulation Without Government: European Biotech, Private Anti-Terrorism Standards, and the Idea of Strong Self-Governance

Stephen M. Maurer[1]

Politicians, scholars, and the general public often dismiss corporate self-governance as inherently weak. The reason, they say, is that it is "voluntary." At the same time, experience with the New Economy suggests that "voluntary" standards can be remarkably mandatory. For example, most consumers buy Microsoft Windows even though – given a choice – they would plainly prefer a different product. Despite this, market forces continue to reinforce Windows' dominance year after year. Similarly, the Worldwide Web Consortium ("W3C") routinely launches new standards over what it terms the "objections of a minority." This strategy works because W3C knows that dissenters will drop their objections once the standards become dominant. In these cases, at least, market forces act more or less like positive law to make self-regulation firm and decisive.

This article asks whether this "strong self-governance" concept can be generalized and, if so, whether doing so is a good idea. It begins with a motivating example. Since 1999, so-called "gene synthesis companies" have specialized in selling artificial DNA to researchers. Shortly after 9/11, industry members began worrying that terrorists could use their products to make weapons. In November 2009, one industry group – International Association Synthetic Biology ("IASB") – announced a Code for screening customer orders. At this point, market forces took over. Within three weeks, more than eighty percent of the industry had endorsed the Code or an equivalent standard, including two companies that had previously tried to block it. These private standards were significantly more stringent than the US government's official "Guidelines."

IASB's Code shows that strong self-governance is feasible and can sometimes yield results that are just as stringent as conventional regulation. This article describes IASB's initiative and the market forces that made it possible. It then argues that similar "strong self-governance" should be possible in many industries. Next, it addresses the much harder question of whether strong self-governance – which

1 Adjunct Associate Professor, Berkeley Law School and Goldman School of Public Policy, University of California at Berkeley, USA. The author wishes to thank the Munich Centre for Governance for hosting a seminar to discuss these ideas in May, 2011. The author also wishes to thank Eugene Bardach, Jens Carsten, Markus Fischer, Andreas Freytag, Rob Van Houweling, Eric Schickler, Tom Slezak, Stefan May, Robert Mikulak, Florian Möslein, and Karl Riesenhuber for their comments and suggestions. Any errors or omissions are due to the author alone.

relies on market forces to suppress dissent – is likely to produce legitimate outcomes. Finally, the article suggests practical steps for governments and private foundations interested in encouraging other industries to practice strong self-governance.

1. Introduction: An Experiment in Governance

Communities almost always pursue collective and/or policy goals through government. However, this method is slow, costly, and tends to empower special interests. Furthermore, government power is limited by national borders and can be hard to enforce in complex environments like markets or universities. Government-to-government treaties can relax some of these limitations at the cost of adding still more time and expense.

Community self-governance offers an alternative. Furthermore, the option is far from theoretical: Indeed, self-governance experiments have occasionally produced spectacular policy interventions in the past.[2] This article reviews the self-governance idea and argues that market forces can sometimes produce "strong self-governance" regimes that are able to exert stringent self-regulation. We also ask whether such methods are likely to produce outcomes that are comparably legitimate to traditional regulation.

We begin with a motivating example. Commercial "gene synthesis companies" first began making artificial DNA molecules to order in 1999. This made many existing genetic engineering experiments easier and opened the door to otherwise impractical projects. At the same time, artificial DNA can be used to make weapons. In 2006, the US government committed itself to developing regulations that would require companies to examine customer orders for potentially dangerous sequences. Remarkably, however, there was also a second track. Many synthetic gene companies see themselves as intellectual heirs to the electronics industry. This includes a long-standing a fascination with internet-style self-governance models. In April 2008, a European trade group known as International Association – Synthetic Biology ("IASB") decided to develop an industry-wide Code of Conduct for screening customer orders. For the next two years, this effort proceeded in parallel

2 The most famous example of community self-governance involves US academic scientists' decision to suppress nuclear fission research in the early 1940s. Significantly, this initiative succeeded despite the US War Department's refusal to participate. Spencer R. Weart."Scientists With a Secret," *Physics Today* 23-30 (Feb. 1976). For more recent experiments in community self-organization, *see* Stephen M. Maurer, "Inside the Anticommons: Academic Scientists' Struggle to Commercialize Human Mutations Data, 1999-2001," *Research Policy* 35:839 (2006) (describing mutations scientists' efforts to organize a self-funding community-wide database), and Stephen M. Maurer, "End of the Beginning or Beginning of the End? Synthetic Biology's Stalled Security Agenda and the Prospects for Restarting It." *Valparaiso Law Review* 45 (4): 1387-1446 (Summer 2011) (describing synthetic biologists' efforts to set standards for academic community). On community self-organization generally, *see* Elinor Ostrom, *Governing the Commons: The Evolution of Institutions for Collective Action* (Cambridge Univ. Press, 1990).

with the US government's regulatory process. This natural experiment provides a unique opportunity for comparing private and public governance side-by-side.

Most observers assumed that they knew how the experiment would end. As the science journal *Nature* argued, private standards could not be trusted:

> As the recent meltdowns on Wall Street have indicated, industry self-policing can sometimes fail dramatically. When bad business practices can have grave effects for the public, regulators should be firm and proactive. The IASB has taken laudable first steps in providing government regulators with guidelines they can build from. Now, the regulators need to act.[3]

Three years later, it is clear that *Nature* was wrong. Indeed, government's own regulations – actually, non-binding "Guidelines" – turn out to be far less "firm" or "proactive" than IASB's Code.

How is this possible? Most self-governance initiatives are meaningless unless the entire community agrees to participate. Conversely, dissenters can usually withhold their consent until the majority agrees to some watered-down, "lowest common denominator" outcome. At the same time, we know that New Economy markets often generate powerful, industry-wide standards. For example, few consumers would willingly choose Microsoft's Windows operating system. Despite this, most continue to purchase it year after year. They do this because the benefits of belonging to a dominant standard – *e.g.* being able to share documents with friends – far outweigh the inherent quality differences between Windows and its competitors. This ultimately persuades most dissenters to drop their objections.

The main novelty in IASB's case, of course, is that organizers were trying to define much more than product characteristics. Instead, they sought to implement industry antiterrorism measures, *i.e.* achieve a public purpose. This, however, turns out to be a distinction without a difference. As discussed in Section 3, large DNA customers strongly prefer a single, industry-wide security standard to multiple conflicting ones. The resulting network effect helped IASB to overcome initial opposition and make its Code the dominant industry standard. More generally, we argue that similar consumer preferences are common. This suggests that IASB-style "strong self-governance" should be possible in many high technology industries.

This article examines the synthetic gene industry's experiment with private screening standards. Remarkably, we will see that IASB's Code was stronger – and also plausibly more democratic – than the federal government's own Guidelines. The balance of the article asks whether strong self-governance is likely to work similarly well in the future. We begin by arguing that the conditions for strong self-governance are present in many high technology industries (Section 6). We then

3 Editorial: "Pathways to Security," *Nature* 455:432.

turn to the much harder question of whether strong self-governance is a good policy option (Sections 7 and 8). We present various arguments suggesting that its outputs can be expected to reflect democratic values at least as well as conventional regulation. We also suggest strategies for combining private and public governance tracks so that – unlike the IASB case – each improves the other (Section 9). Section 10 identifies policy interventions that government can use to promote future self-governance experiments. Section 11 provides a brief conclusion.

2. Strong Self-Governance

There is now a large literature on governance, *i.e.* the idea that policymaking and regulation are increasingly performed by networks that include private parties.[4] But this suggests the further question of whether governance networks can consist *entirely* of private parties.[5] Here, the main theoretical contribution comes from contract governance scholars, who point out that private parties often agree to replace public law with what amount to private statutes. Traditionally, most of these agreements have been limited to narrowly economic activities like defining shareholder rights[6] or arbitrating transnational business disputes.[7] Still, there are also examples in which corporations have developed private codes to address product safety, pollution, public health, and other topics more normally associated with formal regulation.[8] So far, most scholars have been skeptical. Self-governance, they argue, is almost always weak and sometimes no better than a public relations exercise.[9] At the same time, the reasons for this criticism are obscure. In particular the usual argument – that business executives oppose regulation for personal economic reasons – seems overly simplistic. The reason is that executive compensation is only very approximately aligned with corporate profits. This gives executives

4 For a recent survey of the governance concept, *see* Arthur Benz, "Governance in Connected Arenas – Political Science Analysis of Coordination and Control in Complex Rule Systems," in Dorothea Jansen, *New Forms of Governance in Research Organizations: Disciplinary Approaches, Interfaces, and Integration* (Springer 2007).

5 For example, Benz remarks that governance can refer both to the "cooperative state" and to "self-regulation of private actors beyond the state or in the 'shadow' of the state." *Id.*

6 *See e.g,* Bruce H. Kobayashi & Larry E. Ribstein, "Law as Byproduct: Theories of Private Law Production," (mimeo) http://escholarship.org/uc/item/9mg4g1dn; Eric Talley and Gillian Hadfield, "On Public versus Private Provision of Corporate Law," *Journal of Law and Economics* 22:414-444 (2006).

7 Dirk Lehmkuhl, "Resolving Transnational Disputes: Commercial Arbitration and Linkages Between Multiple Providers of Governance Services" pp. 101-124 in Mathias Koenig-Archibugi and Michael Zurn, *New Modes of Governance in the Global System: Exploring Publicness, Delegation and Inclusiveness* (Palgrave 2006).

8 Daniel J. Fiorino, "Voluntary Initiatives, Regulation, and Nanotechnology Oversight: Charting a Path"
Working Paper: Project on Emerging Nanotechnologies No. 19. (2010)
http://www.nanotechproject.org/publications/archive/voluntary/; *see also,* Stephen M. Maurer, "Five Easy Pieces: Case Studies of Entrepreneurs Who Organized Private Communities for a Public Purpose," (George Washington University Law School Conference Paper: 2010) http://papers.ssrn.com/sol3/papers.cfm?abstract_id=1713329.

9 Bowman, Diana M., and Graeme A. Hodge. "Counting on Codes: An Examination of Transnational Codes as a Regulatory Governance Mechanism for Nanotechnologies." *Regulation &Governance* 3:145-164 at 155.

considerable room to act on conscience.[10] Why, then, should self-governance be weak?

This section reviews conventional self-governance and presents three arguments for its weakness. We then ask how New Economy-style market forces can evade these limits to establish a qualitatively new, strong self-governance regime.

Ordinary Self-Regulation. Self-governance typically consists of a political process in which organizers try to persuade all or nearly all community members to consent to a common standard.[11] However, this scenario immediately implies three substantial handicaps. First, organizers must contact and persuade each member separately. This implies that time and expense scale with community size. This task quickly becomes daunting for communities that include more than a few hundred members.[12] Second, most public policy goals require at least approximate unanimity.[13] This gives dissenters a veto. If this veto is also costless, dissenters can block community action indefinitely until organizers water down their standard to some "lowest common denominator" outcome.[14] Finally, market forces tend to destabilize any standard that requires significant expense. As Grant McConnell remarked fifty years ago, competitive markets do not permit companies to take on unnecessary costs.[15] This makes even unanimous agreements vulnerable to new entrants and/or cheating by incumbents.

10 The notion that business executives invariably oppose regulation also contradicts everyday experience. After all, most of us have met executives who claim to favor significant regulation. Over the past five years, I have repeatedly heard gene synthesis executives express such opinions in both private and public settings. Furthermore, these opinions were obviously sincere. Indeed, IASB's Code could never have happened otherwise.

11 *See,* for example, the self-governance examples referenced at note 2, *supra.*

12 For a discussion of how organizers tried to organize a very large community comprised of more than six hundred mutations biologists, *see* Maurer, "Inside the Anticommons," *supra* at note 2. Significantly, the organizers did not even try to contact each member individually. Instead, they focused on the hundred or so members who attended meetings or otherwise expressed interest. They also encouraged prominent scientists to act as "trusted intermediaries," *i.e.* urge their colleagues to accept the project on faith. In the end, these tactics were only partially successful. *Id.*

13 For example, the refusal of even one company to screen DNA orders would radically reduce the value of private screening. At the same time, many standards are useful even without unanimity. For example, many authors have argued that biologists should obtain independent outside advice before performing "experiments of concern" that could inadvertently produce better weapons technologies. Here, a standard that "only" includes fifty percent of all researchers still cuts the risk in half.

14 This explains the usual scholarly instinct that "[I]ndustry is only likely to engage in collective action if confronted with a credible legislative threat or the 'shadow' of hierarchy. In other words, governments have to exert some pressure before industry takes the necessary self-regulatory step." Adrienne Héritier and Dirk Lehmkuhl, "Governing in the Shadow of Hierarchy: New Modes of Governance in Reguation," in Adrienne Héritier and Martin Rhodes (eds). *New Modes of Governance in Europe: Governing in the Shadow of Hierarchy* (Palgrave 2011).

15 Grant McConnell, *Steel and the Presidency – 1962* (Norton: 1963).

Strong Self-Governance. These arguments against self-governance seem quite general. Crucially, however, they all assume that dissent is costless. In fact, many markets violate this standard. Consider, for example, the case of Microsoft Windows. Most consumers claim that – given a choice – they would purchase a different product. That, however, would eliminate their ability to share files. Furthermore, this penalty is substantial and increases with the number of Windows users. This implies a rich-get-richer principle – more formally a "network effect" – in which consumers choose a standard simply because other consumers have done so before. The result, famously, is a "tipping dynamic" in which small initial popularity differences are rapidly amplified until one standard dominates the market.[16]

Could similar market dynamics support self-governance? There is already one example. The WorldWideWeb Consortium ("W3C") sets Internet standards by asking a self-described "philosopher-king" to build consensus within the community. Crucially, however, the king does not even try to achieve unanimity. Instead, he only builds consensus to the point where the standard can "go ahead despite objections of a minority."[17] After that, market forces punish dissenters until they abandon their objections.

Strong self-governance generalizes the W3C example by arguing that organizers in many high technology markets need only (a) persuade a critical mass of like-minded supporters to adopt the desired standard, and then (b) wait for market forces to do the rest. This immediately removes all three of our arguments against traditional self-governance. First, organizers face much lower costs, particularly if the "critical mass" of required supporters is low.[18] Second, dissenters' consent becomes unnecessary. At this point, "lowest common denominator" effects disappear so that strong standards are possible. Finally, we expect even stringent standards to be stable against market forces. This is because consumers derive real value from having products made under the shared standard. And this lets suppliers raise prices enough to pay for their compliance costs.

All of this, of course, assumes the existence of a "network effect" or, more concretely, that consumers derive value from the existence of a single shared standard. In our Windows and W3C examples this consumer preference was utilitarian and based on interoperability. However, there is no reason why consumers cannot be equally moved by political and/or public relations benefits. We will see in Section

16 For the standard account of "network markets" see Hal Varian and Carl Shapiro, *Information Rules: A Strategic Guide to the Network Economy* (Harvard Bus. School Press: 1998).

17 Tim Berners-Lee, *Weaving the Web,* (HarperCollins: 1999) at 110.

18 The same economic logic was implicit in Berners-Lee's successful efforts to organize the World Wide Web. At some point, Berners-Lee recalls, the early difficult work of political organizing ("pushing the sled") led to self-sustaining cycle in which Web growth made the Web more attractive and produced still more growth. At this point, the Web basically organized itself so that Berners-Lee only needed to steer. *Id.*

3 that large pharmaceutical houses – and many other businesses – insist that they only do business with "ethical" suppliers. But in that case, how can suppliers show that they are ethical? By far the easiest and most obvious strategy is to adopt best practices, *i.e.* do exactly what every other company does.[19] This, however, requires a single industry-wide standard. Conversely, industries with multiple, conflicting standards will usually attract controversy. Here, then, is a classic network effect: The more companies adopt a standard, the more consumers value it and the more costly dissent becomes.

That said, the idea of "strong self-governance" comes at a price. First, the concept is closely related to private sector "standards wars." These notoriously rough-and-tumble affairs are highly unpredictable and generate winners almost at random. For this reason, we can only expect winning standards to reflect the industry's mainstream opinion on average. In specific cases, the results will likely be variable. Second, using market forces to suppress dissent is troubling. Classical contract governance usually proceeds by unanimous agreements that include each affected party. Assuming that actors behave rationally, this can only improve welfare.[20] Strong self-governance, on the other hand, lets majorities force their preferences onto dissenters and/or third parties. This suggests that we should only embrace strong self-governance if its outcomes are approximately democratic, *i.e.* reflect the average citizen's values at least as well as conventional regulation. We return to this point in Sections 7-9.

19 In principle, controversy can also be minimized if the industry pursues a "conspiracy of silence" and adopts no standard at all. This situation quickly becomes untenable, however, as soon as one company starts to propose standards.

20 Gralf-Peter Calliess & Moritz Renner, "Transnationalizing Private Law," *The German Law Journal* 10:1341-1356, 1343 (2009). (Remarking that commercial law "may just as well be performed by private governance regimes" but that the situation becomes "considerably more complicated" where transactions affect the public interest").

3. Synthetic Genes: Community, Customers, Security Choices

Strong self-governance requires specific market conditions. This section introduces the synthetic gene industry and its customers. We also summarize the technology options for screening customer orders.

Community. The first gene synthesis companies opened for business in 1999. By 2007, there were about fifty gene companies worldwide. Most of these were located in the US, Germany, and China.[21] More recently, however, competition has forced companies to automate production that used to be done by hand. This requires large investments and high sales volumes.[22] For this reason, small companies are increasingly diversifying their activities away from gene synthesis or leaving the industry. As a result, the industry is becoming increasingly concentrated. Today, four companies – Geneart, DNA2.0, Blue Heron, and IDT – claim that they possess about eighty percent of the industry's installed capacity. Geneart is a German firm; the others are American.[23]

The average artificial DNA order costs about $10,000 and can be shipped worldwide at negligible expense. This means that all gene synthesis companies sell to the same customers in the same global market.[24] Furthermore, they must satisfy the same customer standards. Significantly, this is true whether the company is located in Shanghai or Regensburg or Iowa.

Customers. Pharmaceutical companies and other large customers know that their suppliers need high sales volume to survive. Indeed, they routinely use this leverage to extract low prices and preferred service. At the same time, they understand that the public worries about high technology and that this could lead to a regulatory backlash against the use of artificial DNA and/or genetic engineering in general. If this happens, pharmaceutical companies will almost certainly sustain far more

21 Garfinkel M, Endy D, Epstein G, and Friedman R. (2007) *Synthetic Genomics: Options for Governance.* Center for Security and International Studies: Washington DC.

22 Stephen M. Maurer, Markus Fischer, Heinz Schwer, Cord Stähler, Peer Stähler, and Hubert S. Bernauer, "Making Commercial Biology Safer: What the Gene Synthesis Industry Has Learned About Screening Customers and Orders" (ITHS Working Paper: 2009) available at http://gspp.berkeley.edu/iths/Maurer_IASB_Screening.pdf.

23 These are not the only large companies. Shanghai-based Shinegene for example, appears to operate a high volume business. Shinegene was one of two Chinese companies to endorse IASB's standard. (Markus Fischer: personal communication).

24 Maurer et al., "Making Commercial Biology Safer," *supra* at note 22. For now, this is only an approximation. However, worldwide trade is already substantial and most observers expect a true global market to emerge in the next decade. *Id.* at 6.

damage than the gene synthesis industry itself.[25] This makes them sympathetic to synthetic gene companies' efforts to self-regulate, whether or not DNA prices rise as a result.

Drugmaker Astra-Zeneca has been particularly active. In 2008, the company announced that it would only do business with suppliers "who embrace standards of ethical behavior that are consistent with our own".[26] Thereafter, company executives attended several key meetings in which gene synthesis companies debated private standards. At the same time, Astra-Zeneca was careful not to endorse any particular standard. Instead, it praised all sides and pressed for a common standard.[27]

Security Choices. Current technology offers two basic screening methods. The first is *human screening.* The process begins by comparing the customer's order against the US government's exhaustive Genbank database. At this point, human experts examine the closest Genbank matches to see whether they are associated with known functions that could pose a threat. This method requires highly-trained workers and can occasionally take up to two hours.[28] The second method is *automated screening.*" Here, companies compare the customer's order against a predefined threat list. This method eliminates the need for human screeners and costs almost nothing. However, it is also less capable. This is because is all existing threat lists are incomplete and will likely remain so for at least a decade.[29]

Most gene synthesis companies introduced some version of routine human screening in the years after 9/11. Strikingly, this expense was even incurred by

25 Synthetic gene revenues pale in comparison to the patent royalties that large drug companies will earn if the technology leads to new therapies. Moreover, large drug companies are much more likely to capture whatever benefits synthetic DNA confers on consumers. *See, e.g.,* Chistopher Paul Milne and Joyce Tait, "Evolution Along the Government-Governance Continuum: Impacts of Regulation on Medicines Innovation in the United States," pp. 107 – 132, 108 in Catherine Lyall, Theo Papaioannou and James Smith (eds.), *Limits to Governance: The Challenge for Policymaking in the Life Sciences* (Ashgate: 2009) at 108 (large pharmaceutical companies own 15% of drug candidates but 70% of all approved drugs).

26 AstraZeneca. "Code of Conduct" (2008) at 4. http://www.astrazeneca.com/Responsibility/Code-policies-standards/Code-of-Conduct.

27 Astra-Zeneca's neutrality offered at least two advantages. First, it kept the company from becoming too closely identified with any particular standard. This shielded it from controversy. Second, Astra-Zeneca had relatively little expertise in biosecurity and/or artificial DNA. From this standpoint, it made sense to let the gene synthesis companies decide. For a counterexample in which large customers actively intervened to set standards for suppliers, *see* Marianne Beisheim and Christopher Kaan, "Transnational Standard-Setting Partnership in the Field of Social Rights: The Interplay of Legitimacy, Institutional Design, and Process Management, pp. 122-144 in Magdalena Bexell and Ulrika Mörth, *Democracy and Public-Private Partnerships in Global Governance* (Palgrave-MacMillan 2010) (private social justice standard for coffee producers).

28 Maurer et al., "Making Commercial Biology Safer," *supra* at note 22 and p. 13. Two hours of expert time represents a substantial expense. Artificial genes typically sell for about $10,000 each. (Markus Fischer, personal communication).

29 Tom Slezak, personal communication.

small companies facing thin profit margins. At the same time, practices differed widely from company to company with persistent rumors that a few companies practiced no screening at all.[30] By early 2008, many industry observers argued that it was time to harmonize industry practice.

30 Maurer et al. "Making Commercial Biology Safer," *supra* at note 22 and pp. 18-21.

4. The Development of Private Screening Standards

Synthetic biologists have discussed the need for community "governance" since the late 1990s. However, the debate gained new urgency after 9/11. In 2006, four large gene synthesis companies – Geneart, Codon Devices, Blue Heron, and Codagenomics – created an International Consortium for Polynucleotide Synthesis ("ICPS") to position themselves at the head of any governance discussions.[31] In addition to developing improved automated screening, ICPS promised to "work with governmental organizations to help facilitate the creation of a governance framework and associated safety protocols to foster an appropriate regulatory environment for the synthetic biology industry."[32] Shortly thereafter, ICPS published a high-profile *Nature Biotechnology* article claiming leadership of what it called "a process for developing effective governance of DNA synthesis technology." The presence of several government co-authors helped solidify this claim.[33] At the same time, ICPS had highly unusual screening preferences. In particular, it focused on cheap automated methods and ignored the human procedures that almost all companies actually relied on.[34] In the end, none of this mattered. The promised governance process never materialized and ICPS dissolved in mid-2009.

This might have been the end of the story. In April 2008, however, the European trade group International Association-Synthetic Biology ("IASB") held a workshop in which members agreed to draft an industry-wide private Code of Conduct at or near the high end of existing practice.[35] IASB members worked on this project for the next fifteen months. The resulting codes were widely distributed throughout industry and government. In July 2009 IASB announced that it would host a meeting to finalize the code later that year. At this point, two of the industry's largest companies – Geneart and DNA2.0 – hastily developed their own competing standard. Unlike IASB, this new standard rejected human screening in favor of auto-

31 Codagenomics has since gone out of business.

32 International Consortium for Polynucleotide Synthesis, http://polysynth.info/.

33 Hans Bügl, John P Danner, Robert J Molinari, John T Mulligan, Han-Oh Park, Bas Reichert *et al.*,"DNA Synthesis and Biological Security," *Nature Biotechnology* 25:627 - 629 (2007). The four FBI agents participated as coauthors in their "individual" capacities. *Id.*

34 *Id.* at 627 (arguing that ultimate solution would involve using "validated software tools to check synthesis orders against a set of select agents or sequences to help ensure regulatory compliance and flag synthesis orders for further review").

35 Hubert Bernauer, Jason Christopher, Werner Deininger, Markus Fischer, Philip Habermeier, Dr. Klaus Heumann, et al. "Technical solutions for biosecurity in synthetic biology," http://www.ia-sb.eu/go/synthetic-biology/activities/press-area/press-information/iasb-report-on-biosecurity-and-biosafety/.

mated solutions based on a predefined threat list. Geneart and DNA2.0 argued that this would be “fast” and “cheap.”[36]

DNA2.0 and Geneart continued to advocate their proposal as late as September 2009. By then, however, they had already joined three other large firms in what they called a “secret pact”[37] to develop yet another private standard. Unlike IASB, this new group – the “International Gene Synthesis Consortium” or “IGSC” – was limited to large companies and explicitly designed to reflect their “perspective” on screening.[38] Its meetings were closed to outsiders.

IASB met in Cambridge, MA. to finalize its Code on November 3. Attendees included representatives from several IASB companies, two IGSC members, an Astra-Zeneca executive, a *Nature* reporter, and various US government officials. By the end of November seven IASB members[39] and two Shanghai-based companies had adopted the Code (Maurer and Fisher 2010). At first, IGSC members declined to say whether they would also join. Two weeks later, however, they announced a competing “Harmonized Protocol.” Unlike the earlier DNA2.0/Geneart proposal, this new document agreed with IASB’s Code of Conduct in all material respects, and included an unqualified adoption of human screening. IGSC members did, however, reserve the right to amend their Protocol in the future.[40]

Three weeks after IASB had announced its Code, more than eighty percent of the industry had either endorsed the new standard or IGSC's functionally equivalent document. Had this process continued, there is no way of knowing how many more companies would have joined the Code or Protocol. Instead, the US government stopped the process. On November 27, it announced draft Guidelines that could be implemented by computer.[41] No company has joined the Code or Protocol since.

36 DNA2.0 presentation slides for FBI “Building Bridges” Conference (on file with the author).

37 Daniel Grushkin, "Synthetic Bio, Meet 'FBIo," *The Scientist* 24:44 (2010). http://www.the-scientist.com/article/display/57355/.

38 *See, e.g.* Erika Check-Hayden, "Gene-Makers Form Security Coalition," *NatureNews* (Nov. 18 2009) http://www.nature.com/news/2009/091118/full/news.2009.1095.htmlhttp:/www.nature.com/news/2009/091118/full/news.2009.1095.html (quoting DNA2.0 CEO Jeremy Minshull: "I think what the IASB is doing is great, but we do have a perspective about the scale of the gene-synthesis industry, which helps us to decide what are practically implementable solutions").

39 Three signatories did not sell artificial DNA. (Markus Fischer, personal communication).

40 International Gene Synthesis Consortium, “Harmonized Screening Protocol.” http://www.genesynthesisconsortium.org/Harmonized_Screening_Protocol.html (2009).

41 US Department of Health and Human Services, "Screening Framework Guidance for Synthetic Double-Stranded DNA Providers," 74 Fed. Reg. at 62,320 (Nov. 27, 2009).

5. The Development of Public Screening Standards

The security concerns surrounding artificial DNA were apparent from the outset and deepened after 9/11. In 2002, the US National Academy of Sciences convened a panel to decide what, if any additional regulations were needed. The panel, in turn, recommended the formation of a special study group – National Science Advisory Board for Biosecurity ("NSABB") – that was organized later that year. In 2006, the NSABB called on the US to develop mandatory regulations explaining what gene synthesis companies should do to screen incoming orders. The Administration met this request by convening an interagency "Working Group" to develop regulations in 2007. Predictably, the Working Group hearings were dominated by large US companies including DNA2.0, Blue Heron, and/or IDT. By comparison, IASB's members were seldom informed of these meetings and, in any case, lacked funds to attend.[42]

Within the Working Group, HHS held lead authority for writing and publishing the regulations. However, the agency was plainly skeptical of regulation. Indeed, it admitted that it was reluctant to impose *any* new costs on industry.[43] This position was clearly unusual. According to the usual justification, government intervenes when self-regulation is inadequate. Here, however, HHS had adopted the opposite principle that regulation should impose no new burdens beyond what industry was *already* doing.[44]

The Working Group published draft regulations – by then downgraded to non-binding "Guidelines" – on November 27, 2009. The centerpiece of the document was a principle called "Best Match" which held that companies should be allowed to fill orders unless the customer's sequence was closer to organisms on the government's so-called Select Agent list than any other Genbank sequence.[45] Like all list-based approaches, Best Match was less capable – but also cheaper – than the private sector's existing reliance on human screeners.

42 The Working Group was, however, aware of IASB's Code initiative from September 2008 onward. The US State Department also interacted with IASB on multiple occasions including the Biological Weapons Convention State Parties meeting in December 2008 and a German Foreign Office meeting in February 2009. (Markus Fischer, personal communication).

43 Meredith Wadman, "US Drafts Guidelines to Screen Genes," *NatureNews* (Dec. 4 2009) ("If the guidance were much more onerous than what providers are currently doing, obviously that might be of some concern").

44 Federal regulation would, of course, still be useful to the extent that it let industry harmonize converge a single standard.

45 The Select Agent list is notoriously *ad hoc* and consists largely of organisms that state programs are thought to have weaponized in the past. *See, e.g.,* National Research Council, *Globalization, Biosecurity, and the Future of the Life Sciences.* (National Academies Press, 2006).

HHS did not finalize the Guidelines for nearly a year. During that time, several scholars published articles complaining that Best Match did nothing to detect threats beyond the Select Agent list and was less capable than either the Code or Protocol.[46] HHS could have readily closed this gap by supplementing Best Match with a human screening requirement. However, the final Guidelines refused to take this step. [47] Even so, HHS made a significant concession. In its original draft, the agency has presented Best Match as a complete solution to the biosecurity problem, *i.e.* making sure that products did not "pose[] a hazard to public health, agriculture, or security."[48] However, the final Guidelines carefully limited themselves to the much narrower and simpler question of whether providers were complying with the Select Agent list. Since HHS admitted that many threats existed outside the Select Agent list,[49] the revised Guidelines said nothing about what additional private standards might be needed.

Prospects. As this article goes to press, the future of screening standards is unclear. With respect to public regulation, HHS plainly admits that the Guidelines are an incomplete solution.[50] Despite this, a US Presidential Commission argued in early 2011 that no further regulation was needed. The future of the IASB and Consortium standards is also uncertain. While the US Guidelines say nothing about non-Select Agents, their enthusiastic endorsement of automated methods could encourage some companies to abandon human screening. This would destabilize the IASB and Consortium standards downward in favor of "fast" and "cheap" solutions. For now, however, the IASB and Consortium standards seem to be holding.

46 *See, e.g.*, Markus Fischer & Stephen M. Maurer, "Harmonizing Biosecurity Oversight for Gene Synthesis," *Nature Biotechnology* 28:20 (2010); Jonathan B. Tucker, "Double-Edged DNA: Preventing the Misuse of Gene Synthesis," *Issues in Science & Technology* (Spring 2010) at 23, http://www.issues.org/26.3/tucker.html; Malcolm Dando, "Synthetic Biology: Harbinger of an Uncertain Future?," *Bulletin of the Atomic Scientists* (Aug. 16, 2010), http://www.thebulletin.org/web-edition/columnists/malcolm-dando/synthetic-biology-harbinger-of-uncertain-future.

47 US Department of Health and Human Services, Screening Framework Guidance for Providers of Synthetic Double-Stranded DNA, 75 Fed. Reg. 62,820 (Oct. 13, 2010).

48 US Department of Health and Human Services, "Screening Framework Guidance for Synthetic Double-Stranded DNA Providers," 74 Fed. Reg. at 62,320 (Nov. 27, 2009).

49 U.S. Dep't Health & Human Services, *Frequently Asked Questions* http://www.phe.gov/Preparedness/legal/guidance/syndna/Documents/synbio-faq.pdf (admitting that "it is not possible at this time to provide a robust database that would identify all or even most dangerous sequences.").

50 US Presidential Commission for the Study of Bioethical Issues, "New Directions: The Ethics of Synthetic Biology and Emerging Technologies" at 73 (2010). http://www.bioethics.gov/documents/synthetic-biology/PCSBI-Synthetic-Biology-Report-12.16.10.pdf.

Indeed, one Consortium member has recently reaffirmed its commitment to human screening.[51]

51 Michael Eisenstein, "Synthetic DNA Firms Embrace Hazardous Agents Guidance But Remain Wary of Automated 'Best Match,'" *Nature Biotechnology:* 28: 1225 -26 at 1226 (2010) (quoting IDT executive Robert Dawson: "There's never a case where we would have a gene go right into production without a human being having looked at both the sequence and the prospective customer.").

6. When Is Strong Self-Governance Possible?

The fact that gene synthesis companies have been able to practice strong self-governance is encouraging. That said, IASB's experience could be an accident. How often should we expect similar results in other industries? We start by noticing that ordinary (*i.e.* weak) self-governance requires two conditions. The first and most obvious is *industry support*. Unlike conventional economic standards, self-governance is a political choice. As such, it ultimately depends on companies' normative beliefs about the value of self-regulation. In our gene synthesis example, most – though by no means all – companies believed that screening was ethically necessary. Absent survey data, it is reasonable to think that executives in many industries would be similarly open-minded. The second condition is *market power*. We have argued that companies in a perfectly competitive market cannot sustain unnecessary costs. For this reason, firms must possess sufficient market power to cover the costs of self-regulation.[52] This requirement, however, will often be satisfied since very few high technology industries compete strongly on price. For this reason, we expect ordinary self-regulation to be possible throughout many if not most bio- and/or high technology industries.

So far so good. However, strong governance invokes a third assumption – Network effects. By analogy with our gene synthesis example, this assumes large customers who are simultaneously (a) sensitive to public opinion, and (b) able to extract substantial concessions from suppliers. This pattern is common for industries that produce inputs for large pharmaceutical and chemical companies.[53] Intriguing examples can also be found in other industries. For example, large retailers Tesco (UK) and Migros (Switzerland) have recently called on their suppliers to implement codes of conduct for nanotechnology products.[54] Similarly, four of the coffee industry's five large purchasers recently endorsed a private social justice code for

52 For a classic statement of this principle, *see* Grant McConnell, *Steel and the Presidency – 1962* (Norton: 1963).

53 For an example of pharmaceutical companies' leverage outside the gene synthesis industry, *see* Cynthia Challenger, "The Balancing Act of Small to Medium Sized Custom Manufacturers," *Chemical Market Reporter* (April 14 2003) (reporting how large customers demand "almost annual price decreases" and free additional services from vendors); Claudia Hume and Bill Schmitt, "Pharma's Prescription," *Chemical Week*, p. 21 (April 11 2001) (reporting producers' claim that competition has cut margins from 15-20% to 10-15%).

54 Stephen M. Maurer, "Five Easy Pieces: Case Studies of Entrepreneurs Who Organized Private Communities for a Public Purpose," (George Washington University Law School Conference Paper: 2010) http://papers.ssrn.com/sol3/papers.cfm?abstract_id=1713329.

their suppliers.[55] In each case, the economic basis for IASB-style strong standards appears to be present.

Deciding whether the conditions for strong self-governance exist will always require an industry-by-industry judgment. That said, the necessary conditions do not seem to be particularly rare or unusual. It is therefore reasonable to think that more self-governance experiments are possible. The next three sections ask whether such experiments are also desirable.

55 Marianne Beisheim and Christopher Kaan, "Transnational Standard-Setting Partnership in the Field of Social Rights: The Interplay of Legitimacy, Institutional Design, and Process Management, *supra* at note 27. The coffee example suggests a second kind of network effect. Interestingly, only two of the industry's five dominant oligopolists originally participated in designing the Code. However, two more have joined since then. Evidently, they found it cheaper to join than to stay out. *Id.*

7. Is Strong Self-Governance Desirable? (Pt. 1): Practicalities

The fact that strong self-governance methods are possible does not make them desirable. We would also like them to generate outcomes that benefit society. We have already remarked that traditional contract governance is almost certainly welfare-improving. This argument, however, is based on the assumption that agreements are voluntary, unanimous, and do not affect third parties.[56] Strong self-governance satisfies none of these assumptions. In our artificial DNA case, for example, the dominant standard emerged over the opposition of two large companies and potentially affects millions of citizens. Such a process is unlikely to be welfare-improving in every case. The question remains, however, whether it is a good idea on average.

This section raises two practical arguments in favor of strong self-governance. The first is that conventional regulation may not be an option. In the case of synthetic DNA, for example, the required multilateral treaty could take a decade or more to negotiate[57] and may not be enforceable even then.[58] In this situation, private standards – however imperfect – will normally be preferable to no regulation at all.

Our second argument invokes what the governance literature calls "output legitimacy."[59] Based on the available evidence, we have good reason to think that IASB's standard reflects popular preferences at least as well as the US government's. This arguably supplies enough legitimacy to try the experiment a second time. And if this second experiment also succeeds, then the case for output legitimacy will be that much stronger.

The problem with output legitimacy, of course, is that it is based on hindsight. We would much rather know whether strong self-governance is a good idea *ex ante*. Section 8 analyzes this problem.

56 This conclusion implicitly relies on consumer sovereignty, *i.e.* the usual assumption that parties are rational and free to determine their own preferences.

57 Bob Mikulak, US Ambassador the Chemical Weapons Treaty (personal communication).

58 US efforts to enforce China's treaty commitments to intellectual property, for example, remain notoriously incomplete. *See, e.g.*, US International Trade Commission, "China: Effects of Intellectual Property Infringement and Indigenous Innovation Policies on the US Economy" (2011). http://www.usitc.gov/publications/332/pub4199.pdf.

59 *See, e.g,*, B. Guy Peters and Jon Pierre, "Public-Private Partnerships and the Democratic Deficit: Is Performance-Based Legitimacy the Answer?" in Magdelena Bexell and Ulrika Mörth (eds.), *Democracy and Public-Private Partnerships in Global Governance* (Palgrave: 2010).

8. Is Strong Self-Governance Desirable? (Pt. 2): Arguments from Theory

Governance scholars frequently point out that "output legitimacy" is not the only approach. Instead arguments can also proceed from "input legitimacy," *i.e.* showing that an extra-governmental institution lets broad constituencies participate in a transparent and procedurally fair way.[60] In our artificial gene case, private standard-setting was open to the entire gene synthesis industry. This notably included many small and/or European companies that had minimal access to US regulators. Further, IASB's procedures were extremely transparent; for example, draft Codes were widely circulated while IASB's meetings were consistently open to all industry members, government representatives, academics, and reporters who cared to attend.[61] Finally, we have emphasized that IASB's Code ultimately emerged from a rough-and-tumble "standards war." While this process made no explicit provision for fairness, it was at least impartial and gave industry members some chance to "vote with their feet" by adopting whichever standard they preferred. Taken as a whole, these factors suggest appreciable input legitimacy and were arguably superior to formal regulation.

This section looks beyond our specific synthetic gene example to ask which groups are generically likely to prevail under private and public standard-setting.

Theory of Strong Self-Governance. There is now a large literature on how consumers' preference for a common standard – "network effects" – operates in the New Economy.[62] To see the main points, imagine a market in which consumers benefit from a shared standard. Further, suppose that this benefit far outweighs any inherent quality difference between standards. Then we expect consumers to pick whichever standard already has the most adherents. This simple model has remarkable implications. First, its rich-gets-richer dynamic implies a so-called "tipping" market: The more popular a standard becomes, the more consumers want to adopt it. Furthermore, we expect small initial differences in popularity to steadily increase until growth becomes explosive. Second, our model exhibits "multiple

60 *Id.*

61 This was in sharp contrast to the Consortium, whose membership was expressly limited to large companies and refused to hold open meetings. It is reasonable to think that aggressive US government "jawboning" could have made the Consortium more transparent and hence more legitimate.

62 *See, e.g,* Hal Varian and Carl Shapiro, *Information Rules, supra* at note 16; Michael A. Katz and Carl Shapiro, "Systems Competition and Network Effects," *Journal of Economic Perspectives* 8:93-115 (1994); Suzanne Scotchmer, *Innovation and Incentives* (MIT Press: 2004).

stable equilibria," *i.e.* almost any standard can potentially rise to dominance. This implies that the winning standard in any particular case is selected at random. Finally, network effects exist throughout the market. For this reason, we expect standards in a worldwide market to ignore national borders.

Extending these ideas to private security standards is straightforward. The only real novelty is that customers' desire for shared standards now is driven by political instead of utilitarian needs.

None of this changes the familiar logic. Thus, we still expect standards to grow explosively once they reach some critical mass. This is nicely illustrated by our gene standards case, in which the IASB standard grew to embrace more than eighty percent of the industry in just three weeks. Similarly, we expect private standards to ignore national boundaries. This was also true of IASB's Code, which quickly spread beyond its European origins to include the US and even China. Finally, we still expect multiple equilibria. Here again, the success of IASB's Code reflects a strong element of chance. For example, it would have been hard to predict that the DNA2.0/Geneart standard would collapse in September 2009.[63]

Fig. 1 translates these ideas into the language of input legitimacy. Here, the horizontal axis reflects a range of regulation preferences ranging from "minimum" to "stringent." Without loss of generality, we make the conventional assumption that average informed opinion is somewhere in the middle. From the standpoint of democracy and legitimacy, we expect ideal regulation to implement this viewpoint. On the other hand, we expect company executives' preferences to be colored by their personal financial interests. For this reason, Figure 1 assumes that industry preferences favor less regulation than the population as a whole. On average, we expect private standards to emerge randomly from the interval marked “Industry Preferences”. This is clearly different from our ideal, pluralist result. We now ask whether government can do better.

63 Following conventional economics usage, we have assumed that network effects are much larger than any inherent differences between the standards themselves. In practice, however, these differences could be substantial. This makes the analysis much more complex. For example, one could argue that companies seeking to avoid criticism will systematically choose strong standards over weak ones. On the other hand, strong standards imply additional costs which may not be sustainable in a competitive market. We will neglect these offsetting effects in what follows.

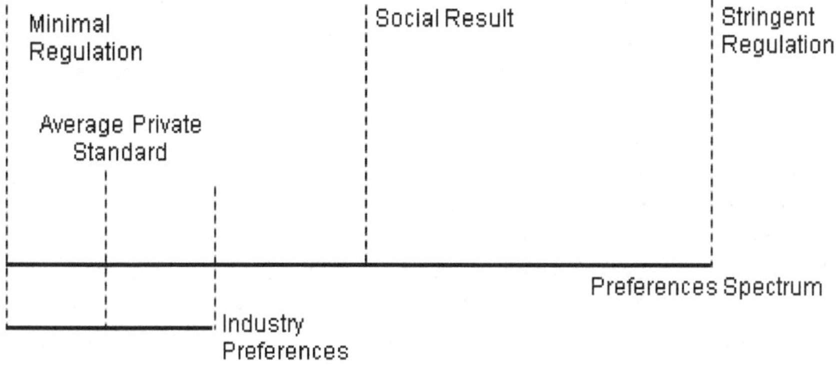

Fig. 1

Theory of Regulation. Political scientists have constructed many different models of regulation over the years. That said, most mainstream models assume that the regulatory agency possesses well-defined policy preferences. (In some theories, the regulatory agency is replaced by an "iron triangle" or "subgovernment" that includes the agency, its clients, and interested legislators.)[64] On the other hand, outside actors can sometimes intervene to overrule the agency's default choice preferences. And even if they do not intervene, the agency may preemptively compromise its preferences to make intervention less appealing.

This discussion leads naturally into the governance literature's "input legitimacy" analysis. Start with the agency's "default choice." Conventionally, we expect the agency to reflect the industry's most extreme views. This is because politicians typically design agencies to lock in "a separately conceived and orchestrated political product, fashioned by a unique coalition of legislators and interest groups, and designed to promote a particular set of interests."[65] This will normally give

64 *See, e.g.,* Jeffrey M. Berry, "Subgovernments, Issue Networks, and Political Conflict" in Richard A. Harris and Sidney Miklis (eds.) *Remaking American Politics.* Westview Press, 1989; Douglas Cater *Power in Washington.* (Random House: 1964); and Ralph Pulitzer and Charles H. Grasty, "Forces at War in Peace Conclave." *The New York Times* (Jan. 18 1919).

65 Terry M. Moe, "The Presidency and the Bureaucracy: The Presidential Advantage," in *The Presidency and the Political System* (5th ed.). (CQ Press:1998). Similar viewpoints can be found, for example, in Berry, "Subgovernments, Issue Networks, and Political Conflict," *supra* at note 64; Harris and Miklis, *Remaking American Politics, supra;* Mathew D. McCubbins, Roger G. Noll and Barry R. Weingast. "Administrative Procedures as Instruments of Political Control." *Journal of Law, Economics, and Organization* 3:243-276 (1987); and Randall B. Ripley and Grace A. Franklin. *Congress, the Bureaucracy, and Public Policy* (The Dorsey Press: 1976).

disproportionate weight to the industry's largest and most active companies.[66] Alternatively, "iron triangle" models assume that the agency shares its power with selected clients and legislators. As in our synthetic DNA example, it is reasonable to expect this group to be skewed in favor of big and/or unusually active companies whose views differ significantly from average industry opinion.

This, of course, is only half the analysis: We have also said that outside groups can intervene. Where intervention is cheap, iron triangles may not form at all. Instead, they degenerate into permanent "issue networks" that include a broad range of viewpoints.[67] Where agencies or subgovernments do exist, their discretion will normally be limited by how efficiently Congress and/or the Executive Branch are able to monitor them.[68] Monitoring, in turn, is typically accomplished by a combination of active surveillance and waiting for citizen complaints.[69] Given that the former is costly,[70] Congressional intervention usually requires constituent complaints (McCubbins *et al.* 1984). These are unlikely to trigger intervention for topics like national security whose constituents are geographically dispersed. By comparison, Executive Branch officials frequently possess significant active monitoring resources and are markedly more sensitive to national political issues than Congress.[71] This suggests that intervention, if it does come, will most likely proceed from the Executive Branch.

66 Once established, this agency culture is amplified through institutional inertia. This can occur for various reasons. For example, officials tend to self-select into agencies they find congenial. Similarly, officials usually find that conforming to agency culture offers significant personal benefits. These include serving personal career ambitions, pleasing co-workers, avoiding emotional conflict, and reducing workloads. *See, e.g.,* James Q. Wilson, *Bureaucracy: What Government Agencies Do and Why They Do It* (Basic Books: 1989).

67 Berry, *supra* at Jeffrey M. "Subgovernments, Issue Networks, and Political Conflict" *supra* at note 64; Richard A. Harris and Sidney Miklis (eds.) *Remaking American Politics*, *supra* at note 64.

68 Brian David Feinstein "Oversight, Despite the Odds: Assessing Congressional Committee Hearings as a Means of Control Over the Federal Bureaucracy." (PhD Thesis: Harvard School of Government: 2009).

69 Mathew D. McCubbins, Roger G. Noll and Barry R. Weingast, "Congressional Oversight Overlooked: Police Patrols versus Fire Alarms." *American Journal of Political Science* 28: 165-179 (1984).

70 Active monitoring is said to be less efficient because Congress must sift through a large number of innocent actions and has limited resources to do so. McCubbins, Mathew D., Roger G. Noll and Barry R. Weingast. "Administrative Procedures as Instruments of Political Control," *supra* at note 65. However, this is only true for the first investigation into a particular topic; once congressional staffers have gained experience the cost of conducting additional investigations falls dramatically. Foreman, Christopher H. 1988. *Signals from the Hill: Congressional Oversight and the Challenge of Social Regulation.* Yale University Press: New Haven CT. This suggests that active monitoring may be important for issues that – unlike artificial DNA screening – Congress has already investigated in the past.

71 McCubbins *et al.*, "Administrative Procedures as Instruments of Political Control," *supra* at note 65.

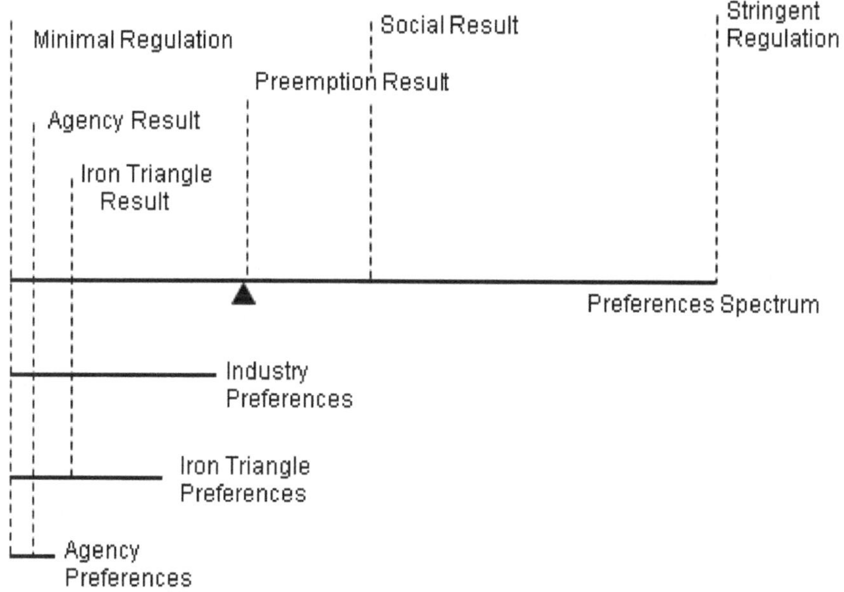

Fig. 2

Figure 2 summarizes these arguments. For the most part, we expect regulatory politics to reflect the normal range of opinion within the intervals marked "Agency Preferences" or, at best, "Iron Triangle Preferences". In either case, these will normally be narrower than average industry opinion. This suggests that private standards will often be at least as democratic as regulatory outcomes. On the other hand, regulatory outcomes can gain input legitimacy to the extent that outside actors potentially and/or actually intervene in the process. This, however, is only likely to happen for relatively incendiary topics. Our synthetic DNA example seems to have been at or near this boundary.[72]

These conclusions are, of course, highly generic. In any particular case we should check to make sure they are realistic, for example by looking at previous regulation to see how nearly the agency resembles a "subgovernment" instead of an "issues network." In the meantime, our analysis strongly suggests that private standards can reflect mainstream opinion at least as well as regulation.

72 Naively, one might have thought that synthetic DNA's combination of futuristic science and biological warfare was incendiary. In practice, this was only marginally true. While extensively covered in *Nature*, the gap between private and public standards was never covered in mainstream media. This may have been a near thing. Reporters for both *The Wall Street Journal* and *60 Minutes* were clearly interested in the story. So, at various times, was the ETC activist group which presumably had its own publicity resources.

9. Is Strong Self-Governance Desirable? (Pt. 3): Procedural Argument

Our final argument for self-governance is procedural. The preceding Sections have tried to compare the "input" and "output" legitimacy of strong self-governance against traditional government. However, this does not matter if we believe in synergy, *i.e.* that strong self-governance improves regulation. Moreover, this scenario has a certain plausibility. In our artificial DNA case, private and public governance each generated important information that the other lacked. For example, the US government clearly possessed superior knowledge of the threat. This could have been readily shared by, for example, expressing a preference between IASB's Code and the much weaker (but also cheaper) DNA2.0/Geneart proposal. Conversely, US regulators seem to have worried that human screening was impractical, unaffordable, and/or would drive US companies overseas.[73] While these arguments were economically doubtful,[74] political hearings were not likely to settle the issue. By comparison, industry's overwhelming decision to adopt private standards built around human screening should have been dispositive.

Information, of course, is not enough. Government must also be prepared to act. This signally did not happen in our gene synthesis case. While the reasons are obscure, they probably stemmed from some combination of iron triangle logic – *i.e.* agency resistance to outside viewpoints – and simple indifference. This suggests that legitimacy can be improved by requiring regulators to engage private standards. This can be done, for example, by enacting regulations that require agencies to (a) comment on the adequacy of any private standard that overlaps their missions, (b) explain why additional public regulation is or is not necessary, and (c) act or build from the private standard as necessary. Similar impact statements are a familiar strategy for forcing agencies to consult groups that they have previously ignored.[75]

73 Meredith Wadman, *U.S. Drafts Guidelines to Screen Genes*, naturenews (Dec. 4, 2009) (quoting NSABB member Stuart Levy "If we deter too much, the gene-synthesis industry will go outside the US and outside our purview, and it will come back to haunt us.")

74 *See, e.g.,* Maurer *et al.*, "Making Biology Safer," *supra* note 22 at pp.9-12.

75 McCubbins et al., "Administrative Procedures as Instruments of Political Control," *supra* at note 65.

10. Next Steps

The preceding sections have argued that strong self-governance is both feasible and desirable. If so, government should encourage additional experiments. In many cases, government's most valuable contribution may be encouragement, *i.e.* reminding industry that self-governance is both possible and praiseworthy. Here, government should be careful to encourage participation by as many companies and viewpoints as possible. Beyond this, government (and especially private foundations) can also promote self-governance by reimbursing industry executives for travel, meeting costs, legal services, and other, similar expenses. In our gene synthesis case, for example, most companies were much more willing to donate executives' time than to supply out-of-pocket expenses. Targeted grants can remove this bottleneck at modest cost.

Government can also reinforce the conditions that make strong self-governance possible in the first place. In particular, it should "jawbone" large customers so that they are more willing to demand ethical standards from suppliers. This indirect pressure will often be more effective than jawboning the suppliers themselves.

In the long run, more ambitious interventions are also possible. In our artificial DNA case, for example, companies practicing the IASB Code or Consortium Protocol have strong financial incentives for recording and sharing their screeners' threat judgments.[76] Indeed, IASB and my University of California group have already created software to do this.[77] At the same time, the resulting database would have many scientific and technical uses beyond screening. This makes it logical for government to fund a central data depository.[78] This would simultaneously reinforce the private standard while encouraging industry to pool data that might otherwise be discarded.

Finally, this article has focused on strong self-regulation in commercial settings. However, the mechanism should work equally well in academic communities. Here, the critical step would be finding public and private funders willing to fill

76 Company screening programs typically find that they have seen three to five percent of all customer sequences before. Where this research is on file, there may be no need to screen orders a second time. These savings can presumably be increased by pooling threat judgments across companies. Maurer et al., "Making Commercial Biology Safer," *supra* at note 22 and p. 24.

77 *Id.* at 24.

78 Similar arrangements in which government supports central facilities that collect contributions from volunteer editors are common in the physical sciences. *See, e.g.* Stephen M. Maurer, "New Institutions for Doing Science: From Databases to Open Source Biology," (European Policy for Intellectual Property Conference: 2003) http://www.merit.unimaas.nl/epip/papers/maurer_paper.pdf.

the crucial "big customer" role. This could readily be done by (a) requiring grant applicants to explain how their proposed experiments conformed to "best practice" biosecurity principles, and (b) rejecting applications that failed to meet this showing. At this point, we would expect community-wide academic standards to emerge in much the same way that IASB's Code did.

11. Conclusion: The Future of Strong Self-Governance

Industry self-governance normally assumes (a) that standards must be unanimous, and (b) that dissent is costless. Historically, these conditions have usually led to weak, lowest common denominator standards. The case is different, however, where consumers prefer a single standard over multiple competing ones. There are at least three reasons for this. First, would-be organizers can succeed without incurring the time and expense needed to contact each community member directly. Instead, they need only persuade some critical mass of members and wait for market forces to do the rest. Second, market forces make dissent costly. This discourages lowest common denominator outcomes and makes strong self-regulation possible. Finally, we normally expect competition to destabilize any private standard that includes substantial compliance costs. This objection fails, however, where industry adoption of a common standard generates new value that consumers are willing to pay for.

IASB's Code shows that strong self-governance is possible and can sometimes produce stronger standards than public regulation. Furthermore, the market forces that led to this outcome are common. This suggests that IASB-style "strong self-governance" regimes can be generalized to other industries. Moreover, government has inexpensive options for encouraging this process.

The question remains whether strong self-governance is a good idea. We have argued that the constituencies that shape private standards are almost always broader than the "iron triangle" coalitions that drive public regulation. On the available evidence, at least, this gives strong self-regulation substantial "input" and "output" legitimacy. At the same time, private and public governance are both highly imperfect. Instead of viewing each channel in isolation, government should find creative ways for them to interact and strengthen each other.

Zeitfracht Medien GmbH
Ferdinand-Jühlke-Straße 7
99095 Erfurt, Deutschland
produktsicherheit@kolibri360.de